A RECORD

OF THE

BATTLES AND ENGAGEMENTS

OF THE

BRITISH ARMIES IN FRANCE

AND

FLANDERS, 1914–1918

By CAPTAIN E. A. JAMES,
48th (South Midland) Divisional Signals T.A.

FOREWORD
BY
LIEUT.-GENERAL Sir HUGH S. JEUDWINE, K.C.B., K.B.E.
(Director-General of the Territorial Army)

THE LONDON STAMP EXCHANGE

Originally Published 1924 by
Gale & Polden Ltd., Aldershot

Reprinted with a new Preface
in 1990 by

THE LONDON STAMP EXCHANGE LTD.
The Military & Naval Book Specialists
5 BUCKINGHAM STREET
STRAND
LONDON WC2N 6BS

Additions Laserset by
Langlands Edition Ltd, Loughborough

Printed by
Antony Rowe Ltd, Chippenham

British Library Cataloguing in Publication Data
James, E. A.
A record of the battles & engagements of the British armies
in France & Flanders 1914-1918.
1. World War I. Western Front. Army operations on
Western Front of World War I. Great Britain. Army
I. Title
940.4144

ISBN 0 948130 18 0

PREFACE TO THE 1990 EDITION

THE LATE Brigadier E. A. James will be well known to students of the Great War as the author of one of the most useful and most used works of reference on that war – *'British Regiments 1914-1918.'* Much less well known, because so long out of print, is this compilation now being reprinted by the London Stamp Exchange after more than sixty five years.

'A Record of the Engagements of the British Armies in France and Flanders, 1914-1918' was prepared by James when he was a young captain, and shows the depth of research and attention to detail that were the hallmark of his later books on the regiments. As Lieut General Jeudwine says in his foreword to the original edition, the book presents in a concise and handy form a record of the part taken by formations, down to brigades, in the Great War. In some minor actions in the early days of the war regiments and battalions are identified.

In 1921 the Battles Nomenclature Committee published their report which formally named all engagements, classified them as battles, actions, affairs etc, and gave the dates of their duration. Without this list, it can be a tedious and uncertain business trying to establish such details, not to mention trying to discover which armies, corps, and divisions took part in which operation – poring through the pages of the Official History, Becke's *'Order of Battle'* or those divisional or other histories that are available.

In this small but invaluable book the author has provided all the answers in a clear and unambiguous way, and as a work of reference it is unique. Every engagement is shown with participating formations, supplemented by explanatory footnotes where appropriate. The two indexes, one of places the other of formations, make it a simple matter to check up any battle or discover which battles any formation took part in throughout the war. The reappearance of this little book will be welcomed by anyone interested in the Great War, be he professional historian or enthusiastic amateur. It is fully deserving of a place on the shelves of military works of reference.

Terry Cave
Worthing, January 1990

FOREWORD

THIS book presents in a concise and handy form a record of the part taken by formations, down to brigades of infantry, in the Great War. Brief as it is, one can well imagine the labour it has cost its author; most of his leisure for the last four years has been devoted to it. Anyone who has attempted to trace exactly the services of even a single division will realize how great his difficulties must have been in recording those of the whole of the British Forces in France and Flanders. He has taken immense pains to make the record accurate, and so far as I have been able to test it I believe he has succeeded admirably. It is a record which will have great value in the years to come, and in my opinion should find a place in every regimental library.

The fact that the author is an officer of the Territorial Army is a welcome sign of the continued interest of its officers in military affairs, and especially in the feats of arms in which the Territorial Force took so glorious a part.

Lieut.-General.

16th February, 1924.

CONTENTS

INTRODUCTION

THIS brochure is an attempt to produce a record of the Armies, Corps, Divisions, and, in certain instances, Infantry Brigades and Battalions engaged in the various Operations, Battles and Actions of the British Armies in France and Flanders during the Great War.

It originally appeared in the form of articles in the "Journal of the Royal United Service Institution" for August and November, 1923, and, as a result of information kindly supplied by readers of the Journal, certain corrections and additions have been made to the original text. Two indexes, one of place names and one of formations, have also been added to facilitate quick reference to any particular engagement or formation.

The framework on which the Record has been built is the Report of the Battles Nomenclature Committee, published in May, 1921, and the names, dates and boundaries fixed in that Report have been carefully followed, with the exception that a few of the names of battles have been slightly changed to agree with the revised official nomenclature used in the lists of Regimental Battle Honours recently announced by the War Office: for example, "Battle of Pozières Ridge" has become "Battle of Pozières."

The work has been compiled from information obtained from many sources and a bibliography would include almost every official publication, formation history, and unit history dealing with the Western Front.

The various types of military operations, in order of importance, have been classified by the Battles Committee as follows :—

1. The "Phase." The war on the Western Front has been divided into seven Phases.

2. "Operations" is the word applied to a series of military events taking place in a certain area and between certain dates having a common purpose or common effect. When an Operation is composed of various Battles, lists of troops engaged are given under the names of the Battles and not under the general heading of Operations. In certain instances, however, Operations do not include any engagements of sufficient magnitude to merit the title of Battle—for example, Operations on the Ancre (11th January-13th March, 1917) ; in such a case a list of formations participating in the Operations is given.

3. The word "Battles" is used in the sense of Group of Battles For example, the Battles of the Somme, 1916, include twelve individual Battles and three Actions. All troops taking part in these separate Battles and Actions are shown under the group title (The Battles of the Somme, 1916) as well as under their individual Battle or Action.

A difficulty presented itself here as a division might come into line on the battle front within the chronological limits of a Group of Battles without participating in any specified engagement. Thus, the 42nd Division was in line east of Ypres from 1st September to 18th September, 1917, without qualifying for any Battle or Action; as this period was not one of trench warfare in the ordinary sense of the word but rather one of consolidation and preparation, essentially part of the Group of Battles, it was decided to include such divisions in a separate list placed immediately after the general list of divisions engaged in the Battles.

In these general lists to Groups of Battles each division's number is followed by a figure in brackets, which indicates the number of individual Battles of the Group of Battles in which the division fought.

4. A " Battle " is one distinct engagement and all formations in line within the official geographical and chronological limits of that Battle are included in the list of troops taking part in that Battle. Certain Battles contain " Tactical Incidents " and the division or divisions taking part in that incident are shown.

5. " Actions " are followed by lists of Armies, Corps and Divisions taking part in that Action, except in Phase I, when the Corps is not shown.

6. " Miscellaneous Incidents " are confined to divisions.

In some cases it was impossible arbitrarily to decide whether a formation qualified for an engagement or not, particularly when the engagement boundary did not coincide with formation boundary; again in some engagements, such as the Battle of Delville Wood, no geographical boundaries have been given, which meant that the greatest latitude had to be given in order to avoid the accidental omission of any formation.

Any foreign troops which were engaged with the British are shown in italics.

In conclusion, the compiler wishes to thank Major A. F. Becke, of the Historical Section (Military Branch), Committee of Imperial Defence, for his invaluable advice and assistance, which enabled the Record to be made sufficiently accurate for publication.

PHASE I.—THE GERMAN INVASION, 1914.

The number of British troops engaged in the operations of this Phase was relatively small compared with the subsequent Phases and, consequently, many of the actions are of greater importance than they would have been had they taken place in later years. For example, during the Retreat from Mons, battalion fights are mentioned, while an attack carried out north of Passchendaele on 2nd December, 1917, by two divisions, 8th and 32nd, is not mentioned in the Report. To preserve a similar balance in the lists of troops engaged in this Phase frequent mention is made of individual Regiments and Battalions and the division to which they belonged is shown in brackets. Corps are not given for the Actions of this Phase.

Operations. The Retreat from Mons (23rd August—5th September, 1914).

BATTLE OF MONS, 23rd—24th August.

Cavalry Division.[1]
I Corps: 1st and 2nd Divisions.
II Corps: 3rd and 5th Divisions.
5th Cavalry Brigade.
19th Infantry Brigade.[2]

With subsidiary—

Action of Élouges, 24th August.

1st and 3rd Cavalry Brigades.
1/Norfolk Regiment and 1/Cheshire Regiment (5th Division).

Rearguard Action of Solesmes, 25th August.

Cavalry Division.
7th Infantry Brigade (3rd Division).
19th Infantry Brigade.

---

[1] The cavalry of the B.E.F. was originally organised as the Cavalry Division, composed of the 1st, 2nd, 3rd and 4th Cavalry Brigades with Divisional Troops, and one independent brigade, the 5th Cavalry Brigade. On 5th September, 1914, the 3rd and 5th Cavalry Brigades were placed under the orders of Brigadier-General H. Gough. On 16th September, 1914, this force was numbered the 2nd Cavalry Division and the 1st, 2nd and 4th Cavalry Brigades became the 1st Cavalry Division.

For full details of the organisation of the B.E.F. in August and September, 1914, *see* Order of Battle, Appendix I, "History of the Great War, Military Operations," Volume I.

[2] The 19th Infantry Brigade began the war as an independent formation. On 31st August, 1914, the 4th Division and this brigade formed the IIIrd Corps. On 11th October, 1914, the 19th Infantry Brigade joined the 6th Division. It served with this Division and with the 27th Division for some time and was finally incorporated in the 2nd Division, where it replaced the 4th (Guards) Brigade, which had gone to the newly formed Guards Division in August, 1915.

Affair of Landrecies, 25th August.

4th (Guards) Brigade (2nd Division).

BATTLE OF LE CATEAU, 26th August.

Cavalry Division.
II Corps: 3rd and 5th Divisions.
4th Division.
19th Infantry Brigade.

Rearguard Affair of Le Grand Fayt, 26th August.

2/Connaught Rangers (5th Infantry Brigade, 2nd Division).

Rearguard Affair of Étreux, 27th August.

15th Hussars (2 troops) (1st Division).
2/Royal Munster Fusiliers (1st (Guards) Brigade, 1st Division).

In the immediate vicinity.

Remainder of 1st (Guards) Brigade (1st Division).
2/Welch Regiment (3rd Infantry Brigade, 1st Division).

Affair of Cérizy, 28th August.

5th Cavalry Brigade.

Affair of Néry, 1st September.

1st Cavalry Brigade.

Troops who arrived and were engaged.

1/Middlesex Regiment (19th Infantry Brigade).

Troops who arrived at Néry after the engagement and troops who were in the immediate vicinity.

4th Cavalry Brigade.
Remainder of 19th Infantry Brigade.
4th Division.

Rearguard Action of Crépy en Valois, 1st September.

13th Infantry Brigade (5th Division).

Rearguard Actions of Villers Cottérêts, 1st September.

3rd Cavalry Brigade.
4th (Guards) and 6th Infantry Brigades (2nd Division).

Operations. The Advance to the Aisne (6th September—1st October, 1914).

BATTLE OF THE MARNE, 1914, 7th—10th September.

Cavalry Division.[1]
Gough's Command.[1]
I Corps : 1st and 2nd Divisions.
II Corps : 3rd and 5th Divisions.
III Corps : 4th Division and 19th Infantry Brigade.

Tactical Incidents :

Passage of the Petit Morin :
Passage of the Marne :

The list of troops engaged for these two Tactical Incidents is exactly the same as that given above for the Battle of the Marne, 1914.

BATTLE OF THE AISNE, 1914, 12th—15th September.

Cavalry Division.[1]
Gough's Command.[1]
I Corps : 1st and 2nd Divisions.
II Corps: 3rd and 5th Divisions.
III Corps : 4th Division and 19th Infantry Brigade.

Tactical Incidents :

Passage of the Aisne and Capture of the Aisne Heights, including the Chemin des Dames.

The list of troops engaged in these Incidents is exactly the same as that given for the Battle of the Aisne, 1914.

With subsequent—

(i) *Actions on the Aisne Heights, 20th September.*

2nd Cavalry Brigade.
I Corps : 1st Division (plus 18th Infantry Brigade attached from 6th Division) and 2nd Division.
II Corps : 3rd Division.

(ii) *Action of Chivy, 26th September.*

I Corps : 1st Division.

Operations. The Defence of Antwerp (4th—10th October, 1914).

Royal Naval Division.

The IV Corps was indirectly concerned with these operations, as the 7th Division (less 21st Infantry Brigade) reached Ghent on 9th October and the 3rd Cavalry Division and 21st Infantry Brigade, 7th Division, arrived at Bruges on the same day.

---

[1] *See* footnote 1, page 1.

Operations. Operations in Flanders, 1914 (10th October—22nd November).

BATTLE OF LA BASSÉE, 1914, 10th October—2nd November.

2nd Cavalry Brigade.
II Corps: 3rd and 5th Divisions.
Indian Corps: Lahore (less Sirhind Brigade) and Meerut Divisions and Secunderabad Cavalry Brigade.

BATTLE OF MESSINES, 1914, 12th October—2nd November.

Cavalry Corps: 1st Cavalry and 2nd Cavalry Divisions.
Ferozepore (7th Indian Infantry) Brigade from Lahore Division.
1/Northumberland Fusiliers, 1/Lincoln Regiment (3rd Division).
2/K.O.S.B., 2/K.O.Y.L.I. (5th Division).
Queen's Own Oxfordshire Hussars.
London Scottish (14/London Regiment).
2/Essex Regiment, 2/R. Inniskilling Fusiliers (4th Division).

BATTLE OF ARMENTIÈRES, 1914, 13th October—2nd November.

III Corps: 4th and 6th Divisions (19th Infantry Brigade in 6th), 3/Worcester Regiment (3rd Division), 1/Dorset Regiment (5th Division).

Tactical Incidents:

Capture of Meteren, 4th Division.

THE BATTLES OF YPRES, 1914,

19TH OCTOBER—22ND NOVEMBER.

Corps: I and IV.

Divisions: 3rd Cavalry (3), 1st (3), 2nd (3), 3rd (1), 7th (2), 7th Infantry Brigade[1] (less 3/Worcester Regiment) and 9th Infantry Brigade[1] of 3rd Division (1), 15th Infantry Brigade[1] (less 1/Norfolk Regiment and 1/Dorset Regiment) of 5th Division (1), 2/K.O.S.B. and 2/Duke of Wellington's Regiment of 5th Division (1) and London Scottish (14/London Regiment) (1).

Also 1st Cavalry Division went into line on 12th November but did not participate in a Battle.

---

[1] The 7th, 9th and 15th Infantry Brigades formed the 3rd Division for this fighting.

(i) BATTLE OF LANGEMARCK, 1914, 21ST—24TH OCTOBER.

I Corps : 1st and 2nd Divisions.
IV Corps : 3rd Cavalry and 7th Divisions.

(ii) BATTLE OF GHELUVELT, 29TH—31ST OCTOBER.

I Corps : 3rd Cavalry, 1st, 2nd and 7th Divisions.

(iii) BATTLE OF NONNE BOSSCHEN, 11TH NOVEMBER.

I Corps : 3rd Cavalry, 1st, 2nd and 3rd Divisions.
7th[1] Infantry Brigade (less 3/Worcester Regiment) and 9th Infantry Brigade of 3rd Division.
15th[1] Infantry Brigade (less 1/Norfolk Regiment and 1/Dorset Regiment) of 5th Division,
2/K.O.S.B. and 2/Duke of Wellington's Regiment of 5th Division.
London Scottish (14/London Regiment).

---

[1] See footnote 1, page 4.

PHASE II.—TRENCH WARFARE, 1914-1916.

Operations. Winter Operations, 1914—15 (November—February).

Defence of Festubert, 1914, 23rd—24th November.

Indian Corps : Meerut Division.

Attack on Wytschaete, 14th December.

II Corps : 3rd Division.

Defence of Givenchy, 1914, 20th—21st December.

Indian Corps : 1st, Lahore, and Meerut Divisions.

First Action of Givenchy, 1915, 25th January.

First Army.[1]

I Corps : 1st Division.

Affairs of Cuinchy, 29th January, 1st and 6th February.

I Corps : 1st Division (29th January), 2nd Division (1st and 6th February).

Operations. Summer Operations, 1915 (March—October).

Battle of Neuve Chapelle, 10th—13th March.

First Army.

IV Corps : 7th and 8th Divisions.
Indian Corps : Lahore and Meerut Divisions.

Action of St. Eloi, 14th—15th March.

Second Army.

V Corps : 27th Division.

Capture of Hill 60, 17th—22nd April.

Second Army.

II Corps : 5th Division.

---

[1] The First and Second Armies were formed on 26th December, 1914, and the Third Army on 11th July, 1915.

THE BATTLES OF YPRES, 1915,
22ND APRIL—25TH MAY.

Army: Second.
Corps: II and V.
Divisions: 1st Cavalry (2), 2nd Cavalry (2), 3rd Cavalry (1), 4th (3), 27th (4), 28th (4), 50th (3), Lahore (1) and 1st Canadian (2), also 13th Infantry Brigade of 5th Division (2).

The 5th Division was within the battle boundaries but did not take part in a battle.

(i) BATTLE OF GRAVENSTAFEL, 22ND—23RD APRIL.

Second Army.

V Corps: 27th, 28th and 1st Canadian Divisions and 13th Infantry Brigade of 5th Division.

Tactical Incidents:
The Gas Attack: 1st Canadian Division.

(ii) BATTLE OF ST. JULIEN, 24TH APRIL—4TH MAY.

Second Army.

V Corps: 2nd Cavalry, 4th, 27th, 28th, 50th, Lahore and 1st Canadian Divisions and 13th Infantry Brigade of 5th Division.

(iii) BATTLE OF FREZENBERG, 8TH—13TH MAY.

Second Army.

V Corps: 1st Cavalry, 3rd Cavalry, 4th, 27th, 28th, and 50th Divisions.

(iv) BATTLE OF BELLEWAARDE,[1] 24TH—25TH MAY.

Second Army.

V Corps: 1st Cavalry, 2nd Cavalry, 4th, 27th, 28th, and 50th Divisions.

BATTLE OF AUBERS, 9th May.

First Army.

Attack on Fromelles.

IV Corps: 7th and 8th Divisions.

Attack at Rue du Bois.

I Corps: 1st and 47th Divisions.
Indian Corps: Lahore and Meerut Divisions.

---

[1] In the Report of the Battles Committee the name of this place is spelt Bellewaerde, but on all Belgian and official maps is spelt Bellewaarde. The second spelling of the word has been used throughout this Record.

Battle of Festubert, 1915, 15th—25th May.

First Army.

I Corps : 2nd, 7th, 47th, 51st[1] and 1st Canadian Divisions.
Indian Corps : Lahore and Meerut Divisions.

Second Action of Givenchy, 1915, 15*th*—16*th June.*

First Army.

IV Corps : 7th, 51st and 1st Canadian Divisions.

First Attack on Bellewaarde, 16*th June.*

Second Army.

V Corps : 3rd Division.

Actions of Hooge, 1915, 19*th and* 30*th July and* 9*th August.*

Second Army.

V Corps : 3rd Division (on 19th July), 14th Division (on 30th July), 6th Division (on 9th August).

The Battle of Loos, 25th September—8th October.

First Army.

I Corps : 2nd, 7th, 9th and 28th Divisions.
IV Corps : 3rd Cavalry, 1st, 15th and 47th Divisions.
XI Corps : Guards, 12th, 21st and 24th Divisions.
Indian Corps[2] : 19th and Meerut Divisions.

With subsidiary :—

(i) *Action of Piètre*, 25*th September.*

First Army.

Indian Corps : Meerut Division.[3]

(ii) *Action of Bois Grenier*, 25*th September.*

First Army.

III Corps[4] : 8th Division.

---

[1] The 51st Division was transferred to Indian Corps on 22nd May.

[2] The Indian Corps, with 19th Division and Meerut Division, came within the battle area north of the La Bassée Canal from 29th September.

[3] The right of the 20th Division, IIIrd Corps, was involved in the attack of the Meerut Division.

[4] Although the 23rd Division was actually holding the line in front of Bois Grenier it does not appear, technically, to qualify for this Action.

(iii) *Second Attack on Bellewaarde, 25th—26th September.*

Second Army.

V Corps : 3rd Division.
VI Corps : 14th Division.

And subsequent—

Actions of the Hohenzollern Redoubt, 13th—19th October.

First Army.

IV Corps : 1st and 47th Divisions.
XI Corps : Guards, 2nd, 12th and 46th Divisions.

Operations. Local Operations, 1916.

Actions of the Bluff, 14th—15th February and 2nd March.

Second Army.

V Corps : 17th Division (14th—15th February).
V Corps : 3rd and 17th Divisions (2nd March).

Actions of St. Eloi Craters, 27th March—16th April.

Second Army.

V Corps : 3rd Division.
Canadian Corps : 2nd Canadian Division.

German Attack on Vimy Ridge, 21st May.

First Army.

IV Corps : 47th Division.

Third Army.

XVII Corps : 25th Division.

BATTLE OF MOUNT SORREL[1], 2nd—13th June.

Second Army.

XIV Corps : 20th Division.
Canadian Corps : 1st Canadian, 2nd Canadian and 3rd Canadian Divisions.

---

[1] Mount Sorrel is 1,200 yards north-east of Hill 60.

PHASE III.—THE ALLIED OFFENSIVE, 1916.

Operations. Operations on the Somme (1st July—18th November, 1916).

THE BATTLES OF THE SOMME, 1916, 1st JULY—18th NOVEMBER.

Armies: Third, Fourth and Fifth[1].

Corps: II, III, V, VII, VIII, X, XIII, XIV, XV, Canadian and I Anzac.

Divisions: 1st Cavalry (1), 2nd Indian Cavalry (2), Guards (2), 1st (5), 2nd (2), 3rd (4), 4th (2), 5th (4), 6th (3), 7th (5), 8th (1), 9th (4), 11th (2), 12th (3), 14th (2), 15th (3), 16th (2), 17th (1), 18th (6), 19th (5), 20th (5), 21st (5), 23rd (6), 24th (2), 25th (4), 29th (2), 30th (2), 31st (2), 32nd (3), 33rd (3), 34th (4), 35th (1), 36th (1), 37th (4), 38th (1), 39th (3), 40th (1), 41st (2), 46th (1), 47th (2), 48th (4), 49th (4), 50th (3), 51st (2), 55th (4), 56th (5), 63rd (1), 1st Canadian (4), 2nd Canadian (4), 3rd Canadian (4), 4th Canadian (3), 1st Australian (1), 2nd Australian (1), 4th Australian (1), and New Zealand (3).

The 5th Australian Division went into line within the limits of the Battles but did not participate in any specified battle.

Total number of divisions engaged: 54 and 2 cavalry.

(i) Battle of Albert, 1916, 1st—13th July.

Fourth Army.

III Corps: 1st, 8th, 12th, 19th, 23rd and 34th Divisions.
VIII Corps: 4th, 29th, 31st and 48th Divisions.
X Corps: 12th, 25th, 32nd, 36th and 49th Divisions.
XIII Corps: 3rd, 9th, 18th, 30th and 35th Divisions.
XV Corps: 7th, 17th, 21st, 33rd and 38th Divisions.

Reserve Army.

This Army took over the VIII and X Corps from the Fourth Army on 4th July, 1916.

Tactical Incidents:

Capture of Montauban: 30th Division.
Capture of Mametz: 7th Division.
Capture of Fricourt: 17th Division.
Capture of Contalmaison: 23rd Division.
Capture of La Boisselle: 19th Division.

---

[1] The Fourth Army was formed on 5th February, 1916, and the Reserve Army on 23rd May, 1916. On 4th July, 1916, during the Battle of Albert, 1916, the latter took over the VIII and X Corps from the Fourth Army. On and after the 30th October the Reserve Army was designated the Fifth Army.

With subsidiary—

Attack on the Gommecourt Salient, 1st July.

Third Army.

VII Corps: 37th, 46th and 56th Divisions.

(ii) BATTLE OF BAZENTIN, 14TH—17TH JULY.

Fourth Army.

2nd Indian Cavalry Division.
II Corps: 1st, 23rd and 34th[1] Divisions.
XIII Corps: 3rd, 9th and 18th Divisions.
XV Corps: 7th, 21st and 33rd Divisions.

Reserve Army.

X Corps: 25th, 32nd, 48th and 49th Divisions.
Tactical Incidents:
Capture of Longueval: 3rd and 9th Divisions.
Capture of Trônes Wood: 18th Division.
Capture of Ovillers: 48th Division.

With subsidiary—

Attack at Fromelles (on the Aubers Ridge), 19th July.

First Army.

XI Corps: 61st and 5th Australian Divisions.

And subsequent—

Attacks on High Wood,[2] 20th—25th July.

Fourth Army.

III Corps: 19th Division.
XV Corps: 5th, 7th, 33rd and 51st Divisions.

(iii) BATTLE OF DELVILLE WOOD, 15TH JULY—3RD SEPTEMBER.

Fourth Army.

XIII Corps: 2nd, 3rd, 9th and 24th Divisions and 53rd Infantry Brigade of 18th Division.
XIV Corps[3]: 20th and 24th Divisions.
XV Corps: 7th and 14th Divisions.

---

[1] The 102nd and 103rd Infantry Brigades of the 34th Division had suffered very heavy losses in the Battle of Albert, 1916. These two Brigades changed places with the 111th and 112th Infantry Brigades of the 37th Division and went into line with the 37th Division, IV Corps, First Army, on Vimy Ridge, while the two Brigades of the 37th Division, mentioned above, fought in the Battle of Albert, 1916, Battle of Bazentin and Battle of Pozières under the 34th Division.

[2] High Wood was finally captured by the 47th Division, III Corps, on 15th September, 1916.

[3] The XIV Corps relieved the XIII Corps at midnight 16–17th August, 1916.

(iv) Battle of Pozières, 23rd July—3rd September.

Fourth Army.

III Corps : 1st, 15th, 19th, 23rd and 34th Divisions.

Reserve Army.

II Corps[1] : 12th, 25th, 48th and 49th Divisions.
X Corps : 12th, 48th and 49th Divisions.
I Anzac Corps : 1st Australian, 2nd Australian, and 4th Australian Divisions.

Tactical Incidents :

Fighting for Mouquet Farm,[2] 12th, 25th, 48th, 1st Australian, 2nd Australian and 4th Australian Divisions.

(v) Battle of Guillemont, 3rd—6th September.

Fourth Army.

XIV Corps : 5th, 16th and 20th Divisions.
XV Corps : 7th, 24th and 55th Divisions.

(vi) Battle of Ginchy, 9th September.

Fourth Army.

XIV Corps : 16th and 56th Divisions.
XV Corps : 55th Division.

(vii) Battle of Flers—Courcelette,[3] 15th—22nd September.

Fourth Army.

1st Cavalry and 2nd Indian Cavalry Divisions.
III Corps : 1st, 15th, 23rd, 47th and 50th Divisions and 103rd Infantry Brigade of 34th Division.
XIV Corps : Guards, 5th, 6th, 20th and 56th Divisions.
XV Corps : 14th, 21st, 41st, 55th and New Zealand Divisions.

Reserve Army.

II Corps : 11th and 49th Divisions.
Canadian Corps : 1st Canadian, 2nd Canadian and 3rd Canadian Divisions.

Tactical Incidents :

Capture of Martinpuich : 15th Division.

---

[1] The II Corps took over the front and divisions in line of the X Corps on 24th July, 1916.

[2] Part of Mouquet Farm was captured by the 3rd Canadian Division on 16th September, 1916, and the Farm was finally captured by the 11th Division on 26th September, 1916.

[3] This battle is particularly noteworthy for two reasons. It was the first occasion on which tanks went into action and was the first day on which British artillery fired a creeping or, as it was then called, rolling barrage.

(viii) BATTLE OF MORVAL, 25TH—28TH SEPTEMBER.

Fourth Army.

III Corps: 1st, 23rd and 50th Divisions.
XIV Corps: Guards, 5th, 6th, 20th and 56th Divisions.
XV Corps: 21st, 55th and New Zealand Divisions.

Tactical Incidents:

Capture of Combles: 56th Division.
Capture of Lesbœufs: Guards and 6th Division.
Capture of Gueudecourt: 21st Division.

(ix) BATTLE OF THIEPVAL, 26TH—28TH SEPTEMBER.

Reserve Army.

II Corps: 11th and 18th Divisions.
V Corps: 39th Division.
Canadian Corps: 1st Canadian, 2nd Canadian and 3rd Canadian Divisions.

(x) BATTLE OF LE TRANSLOY, 1ST—18TH OCTOBER.

Fourth Army.

III Corps: 9th, 15th, 23rd, 47th and 50th Divisions.
XIV Corps: 4th, 6th, 20th and 56th Divisions.
XV Corps: 12th, 21st, 30th, 41st and New Zealand Divisions and 88th Infantry Brigade of 29th Division.

Reserve Army.

Canadian Corps: 1st Canadian, 2nd Canadian, 3rd Canadian and 4th Canadian Divisions.

Tactical Incidents:

Capture of Eaucourt l'Abbaye: 47th Division.
Capture of Le Sars: 23rd Division.
Attacks on the Butte de Warlencourt[1]: 9th, 15th, 23rd and 47th Divisions.

(xi) BATTLE OF THE ANCRE HEIGHTS, 1ST OCTOBER—11TH NOVEMBER.

Reserve Army.

II Corps: 18th, 19th, 25th, 39th[2] and 4th Canadian[3] Divisions.
V Corps: 39th Division.

---

[1] The 48th and 50th Divisions came in after the end of the Battle of Le Transloy and carried out attacks on the Butte de Warlencourt.

[2] The 39th Division was transferred from the V Corps to the II Corps on 4th October, 1916.

[3] The 4th Canadian Division was transferred from the Canadian Corps to the II Corps on 17th October, 1916, when the Canadian Corps was withdrawn from the battle front.

Canadian Corps: 1st Canadian, 2nd Canadian, 3rd Canadian and 4th Canadian Divisions.[1]

Tactical Incidents:

Capture of Schwaben Redoubt: 18th and 39th Divisions.
Capture of Stuff Redoubt[2]: 25th Division.
Capture of Regina Trench: 18th, 25th, 39th and 4th Canadian Divisions.

(xii) BATTLE OF THE ANCRE, 1916, 13TH—18TH NOVEMBER.

Fourth Army.

III Corps: 48th Division.

Fifth Army.

II Corps: 18th, 19th, 39th and 4th Canadian Divisions.
V Corps: 2nd, 3rd, 32nd, 37th, 51st and 63rd Divisions.
XIII Corps: 31st Division and 120th Infantry Brigade of 40th Division.

Tactical Incidents:

Capture of Beaumont Hamel: 51st Division.

---

[1] *See* footnote 3, page 13.

[2] The 11th Division had gained a footing in the Stuff Redoubt in the fighting at the end of September.

PHASE IV.—THE ADVANCE TO THE HINDENBURG LINE, 1917.

As there were no Battles in this Phase, a general list of formations engaged in the Operations is given, as explained in the Introduction.

Operations. Operations on the Ancre (11th January—13th March, 1917).

Fifth Army.

II Corps: 2nd, 18th and 63rd Divisions.
IV Corps: 2nd, 11th, 51st and 61st Divisions.
V Corps: 7th, 19th, 31st, 32nd, 46th and 62nd Divisions.
I Anzac Corps: 1st Australian, 2nd Australian, 4th Australian and 5th Australian Divisions.

Actions of Miraumont, 17th—18th February.

Fifth Army.

II Corps: 2nd, 18th and 63rd Divisions.

Capture of the Thilloys, 25th February—2nd March.

Fifth Army.

II Corps: 2nd Division.
I Anzac Corps: 1st Australian, 2nd Australian, and 5th Australian Divisions.

Capture of Irles, 10th March.

Fifth Army.

II Corps: 2nd and 18th Divisions.
I Anzac Corps: 2nd Australian Division.

Operations. German Retreat to the Hindenburg Line (14th March—5th April, 1917).

Third Army.

VII Corps: 14th, 21st, 30th and 56th Divisions.

Fourth Army.

5th Cavalry Division.[1]
III Corps: 1st, 48th and 59th Divisions.
IV Corps: 32nd, 35th and 61st Divisions.
XIV Corps: Guards and 20th[2] Divisions.
XV Corps: 8th, 20th and 40th Divisions.

Fifth Army.

4th Cavalry Division.[1]
II Corps: 2nd and 18th Divisions.
V Corps: 7th, 46th and 62nd Divisions.
XVIII Corps: 58th Division.
I Anzac Corps: 2nd Australian, 4th Australian and 5th Australian Divisions.

Capture of Bapaume, 1917, *17th March.*

Fifth Army.

I Anzac Corps: 2nd Australian Division.

Occupation of Péronne, 18*th March.*

48th Division (III Corps).

---

[1] The 1st and 2nd Indian Cavalry Divisions became the 4th and 5th Cavalry Divisions on 26th November, 1916.

[2] The 20th Division was transferred from XIV Corps to XV Corps on 25th March, 1917.

PHASE V.—THE ALLIED OFFENSIVES, 1917.

Operations. The Arras Offensive (9th April—15th May, 1917).

THE BATTLES OF ARRAS, 1917, 9TH APRIL—4TH MAY.

Armies: First and Third.

Corps: Cavalry, I, VI, VII, XIII, XVII and Canadian.

Divisions: 1st Cavalry (1), 2nd Cavalry (1), 3rd Cavalry (1), 2nd (3), 3rd (4), 4th (2), 5th (3), 9th (2), 12th (3), 14th (2), 15th (2), 17th (2), 18th (1), 21st (2), 24th (1), 29th (2), 30th (2), 31st (1), 33rd (1), 34th (3), 37th (3), 50th (2), 51st (2), 56th (2), 63rd (2), 1st Canadian (3), 2nd Canadian (4), 3rd Canadian (3), and 4th Canadian (1).

Total number of divisions engaged: 26 and 3 cavalry.

(i) BATTLE OF VIMY, 1917, 9TH—14TH APRIL.

First Army.

I Corps: 24th Division.

Canadian Corps: 5th, 1st Canadian, 2nd Canadian, 3rd Canadian and 4th Canadian Divisions.

FIRST BATTLE OF THE SCARPE, 1917, 9TH—14TH APRIL.

First Army.

XIII[1] Corps: 2nd Division.

Third Army.

Cavalry Corps: 1st Cavalry, 2nd Cavalry and 3rd Cavalry Divisions.

VI Corps: 3rd, 12th, 15th, 17th, 29th and 37th Divisions.

VII Corps: 14th, 21st, 30th, 50th and 56th Divisions.

XVII Corps: 4th, 9th, 34th and 51st Divisions.

Tactical Incidents:

Capture of Monchy le Preux: 3rd Cavalry and 37th Divisions.

Capture of Wancourt Ridge: 50th Division.

(ii) SECOND BATTLE OF THE SCARPE, 1917, 23RD—24TH APRIL.

First Army.

XIII Corps: 63rd Division.

Third Army.

VI Corps: 15th, 17th and 29th Divisions and 8th Infantry Brigade of 3rd Division.

VII Corps: 30th, 33rd and 50th Divisions.

---

[1] The XIII Corps came into line on the 12th April, 1917, when the 2nd Division relieved the 51st Division, XVII Corps.

XVII Corps: 37th and 51st Divisions and 103rd Infantry Brigade of 34th Division.

Tactical Incidents:

Capture of Guémappe: 15th Division.
Capture of Gavrelle: 63rd Division.

With subsidiary—

Attack on La Coulotte, 23rd April.

First Army.

Canadian Corps: 5th, 2nd Canadian and 3rd Canadian Divisions.

(iii) BATTLE OF ARLEUX, 28TH—29TH APRIL.

First Army.

XIII Corps: 2nd and 63rd Divisions.
Canadian Corps: 1st Canadian and 2nd Canadian Divisions.

Third Army.

VI Corps: 3rd and 12th Divisions.
XVII Corps: 34th and 37th Divisions.

(iv) THIRD BATTLE OF THE SCARPE, 1917, 3RD—4TH MAY.

First Army.

XIII Corps: 2nd, 5th and 31st Divisions.
Canadian Corps: 1st Canadian, 2nd Canadian and 3rd Canadian Divisions.

Third Army.

VI Corps: 3rd, 12th and 56th Divisions.
VII Corps: 14th, 18th and 21st Divisions.
XVII Corps: 4th and 9th Divisions.

Tactical Incidents:

Capture of Fresnoy: 1st Canadian Division.

With subsequent—

(i) *Capture of Rœux, 13th—14th May.*

Third Army.

VI Corps: 3rd and 12th Divisions.
XVII Corps: 17th and 51st Divisions.

(ii) *Capture of Oppy Wood, 28th June.*

First Army.

XIII Corps: 5th and 31st Divisions.

Operations. Flanking Operations to the Arras Offensive.

(*a*) Round Bullecourt (11th April—16th June).

Fifth Army.

V Corps: 7th, 58th and 62nd Divisions.
I Anzac Corps: 1st Australian, 2nd Australian, 4th Australian and 5th Australian Divisions.

First Attack on Bullecourt, 11th April.

Fifth Army.

V Corps: 62nd Division.
I Anzac Corps: 4th Australian Division.

German Attack on Lagnicourt, 15th April.

Fifth Army.

V Corps: 62nd Division.
I Anzac Corps: 1st Australian and 2nd Australian Divisions.

BATTLE OF BULLECOURT, 3rd—17th May.

Fifth Army.

V Corps: 7th, 58th and 62nd Divisions.
I Anzac Corps: 1st Australian, 2nd Australian and 5th Australian Divisions.

Actions on the Hindenburg Line,[1] *20th May—16th June.*

Third Army.

VII Corps: 21st and 33rd Divisions.

Fifth Army.

V Corps[2]: 7th, 58th and 62nd Divisions.
I Anzac Corps[2]: 5th Australian Division.
IV Corps[2]: 20th Division.

---

[1] It appears that the north boundary of these actions should have been the Sensée River instead of the Ecoust St. Mein Road. The main feature of these actions was the attack of the 33rd Division on the Hindenburg Line between Bullecourt and the Sensée River; that is, outside the official battle area. The 33rd and 21st Divisions, which fought on this portion of the front, have been included in the list.

[2] Considerable changes in the higher formations took place during this fighting. At 10 a.m., 26th May, the IV Corps and 20th Division relieved the I Anzac Corps and the 5th Australian Division, and at 10 a.m. on 31st May the Third Army took over the IV and V Corps from the Fifth Army.

(*b*) Towards Lens (3rd June—26th August).

First Army.

I Corps: 6th and 46th Divisions.
Canadian Corps: 1st Canadian, 2nd Canadian, 3rd Canadian and 4th Canadian Divisions.

Affairs south of the Souchez River, 3rd—25th June.

First Army.

Canadian Corps: 3rd Canadian and 4th Canadian Divisions.

Capture of Avion, 26th—29th June.

First Army.

Canadian Corps: 3rd Canadian and 4th Canadian Divisions.

BATTLE OF HILL 70, 15th—25th August.

First Army.

I Corps: 6th and 46th Divisions.
Canadian Corps: 1st Canadian, 2nd Canadian, 3rd Canadian and 4th Canadian Divisions.

Operations. The Flanders Offensive (7th June—10th November, 1917).

THE BATTLE OF MESSINES, 1917, 7th—14th June.

Second Army.

IX Corps: 11th, 16th, 19th and 36th Divisions.
X Corps: 23rd, 24th, 41st and 47th Divisions.
II Anzac Corps[1]: 25th, 3rd Australian, 4th Australian and New Zealand Divisions.

Tactical Incidents:

Capture of Wytschaete: 16th and 36th Divisions.

German Attack on Nieuport, 10th—11th July.

Fourth Army.

XV Corps: 1st and 32nd Divisions.

---

[1] The southern portion of the II Anzac Corps front was held by two battalions of the 170th Infantry Brigade, 57th Division, under 3rd Australian Division from 7th to 10th June and from then until the end of the battle by the 4th New Zealand Infantry Brigade under 3rd Australian Division to 12th June, then under New Zealand Division.

THE BATTLES OF YPRES, 1917,[1]
31ST JULY—10TH NOVEMBER.

Armies: Second and Fifth.
Corps: II, V, IX, X, XIV, XVIII, XIX, Canadian, I Anzac and II Anzac.
Divisions: Guards (4), 1st (1), 3rd (2), 4th (4), 5th (4), 7th (4), 8th (2), 9th (2), 11th (4), 14th (3), 15th (2), 16th (1), 17th (2), 18th (4), 19th (6), 20th (3), 21st (3), 23rd (4), 24th (2), 25th (1), 29th (5), 30th (1), 33rd (2), 35th (1), 36th (1), 37th (6), 38th (2), 39th (5), 41st (2), 48th (4), 49th (1), 50th (1), 51st (2), 55th (2), 56th (1), 57th (1), 58th (3), 59th (2), 61st (1), 63rd (1), 66th (1), 1st Canadian (1), 2nd Canadian (1), 3rd Canadian (1), 4th Canadian (1), 1st Australian (5), 2nd Australian (5), 3rd Australian (3), 4th Australian (3), 5th Australian (4), and New Zealand (3).
The 34th, 42nd and 47th Divisions went into line on the battle front, but did not take part in any specified battle.
Total number of divisions engaged: 54

(i) Battle of Pilckem, 31st July—2nd August.

Second Army.

X Corps: 41st Division.

Fifth Army.

II Corps: 8th, 24th, 25th and 30th Divisions and 53rd Infantry. Brigade, 18th Division.
XIV Corps: Guards and 38th Divisions.
XVIII Corps: 39th and 51st Divisions.
XIX Corps: 15th and 55th Divisions.

With subsequent—

Capture of Westhoek, 10th August.

Fifth Army.

II Corps: 18th and 25th Divisions.

(ii) Battle of Langemarck, 1917, 16th—18th August.

Second Army.

X Corps: 39th Division.

---

[1] The Battles Nomenclature Committee has defined a common geographical boundary for the eight individual battles of the Battles of Ypres, 1917, and the compiler has adhered to this boundary in deciding which formations qualify for the various battles, although, in several cases, it meant the inclusion of troops which did not actually attack. It would have been more satisfactory if a separate geographical boundary had been assigned to each battle. as was done for the Battles of the Somme, 1916.

Fifth Army.

II Corps: 8th, 14th, 24th and 56th Divisions and 53rd Infantry Brigade, 18th Division.
XIV Corps: 20th, 29th and 38th Divisions.
XVIII Corps: 11th and 48th Divisions.
XIX Corps: 15th, 16th, 36th and 61st Divisions.

(iii) [1]Battle of the Menin Road, 20th—25th September.

Second Army.

IX Corps: 19th and 37th Divisions.
X Corps: 23rd, 33rd, 39th and 41st Divisions.
I Anzac Corps: 1st Australian, 2nd Australian, 4th Australian and 5th Australian Divisions.

Fifth Army.

V Corps: 3rd, 9th, 55th and 59th Divisions.
XIV Corps: Guards, 20th and 29th Divisions.
XVIII Corps: 51st and 58th Divisions.

(iv) Battle of Polygon Wood, 26th September—3rd October.

Second Army.

IX Corps: 19th and 37th Divisions.
X Corps: 5th, 7th, 21st, 23rd, 33rd and 39th Divisions.

---

[1] The Fifth Army carried out three minor operations in the latter part of August which are not mentioned in the Official Battle List. The following extract from paragraph 48 of Lord Haig's Despatch, dated 25th December, 1917, deals with these operations:—

" . . . on 19th, 22nd and 27th August, positions of considerable local importance in the neighbourhood of St. Julien were captured with some hundreds of prisoners, as the result of minor attacks, conducted under the most unfavourable conditions of ground and weather. The ground gained represented an advance of about 800 yards on a front of over two miles."

The troops of Fifth Army engaged were

19th August.

XVIII Corps: 11th and 48th Divisions.

22nd August.

II Corps: 14th and 47th Divisions.
XVIII Corps: 11th and 48th Divisions.
XIX Corps: 15th and 61st Divisions.

27th August.

XIV Corps: 38th Division.
XVIII Corps: 11th and 48th Divisions.
XIX Corps: 61st Division.

I Anzac Corps : 1st Australian, 2nd Australian, 4th Australian and 5th Australian Divisions.
II Anzac Corps[1] : 3rd, 59th, 3rd Australian and New Zealand Divisions.

Fifth Army.

V Corps : 3rd and 59th Divisions.
XIV Corps : 4th, 20th and 29th Divisions.
XVIII Corps : 11th, 48th and 58th Divisions.

(v) Battle of Broodseinde, 4th October.

Second Army.

IX Corps : 19th and 37th Divisions.
X Corps : 5th, 7th and 21st Divisions.
I Anzac Corps : 1st Australian and 2nd Australian Divisions.
II Anzac Corps : 3rd Australian and New Zealand Divisions.

Fifth Army.

XIV Corps : 4th and 29th Divisions.
XVIII Corps : 11th and 48th Divisions.

(vi) Battle of Poelcappelle, 9th October.

Second Army.

IX Corps : 19th and 37th Divisions.
X Corps : 5th and 7th Divisions.
I Anzac Corps : 1st Australian and 2nd Australian Divisions.
II Anzac Corps : 49th and 66th Divisions.

Fifth Army.

XIV Corps : Guards, 4th and 29th Divisions.
XVIII Corps : 11th and 48th Divisions.

(vii) First Battle of Passchendaele, 12th October.

Second Army.

IX Corps : 19th and 37th Divisions.
X Corps : 14th and 23rd Divisions.
I Anzac Corps : 4th Australian and 5th Australian Divisions.
II Anzac Corps : 3rd Australian and New Zealand Divisions.

Fifth Army.

XIV Corps : Guards, 4th and 17th Divisions.
XVIII Corps : 9th and 18th Divisions.

---

[1] The II Anzac Corps relieved the V Corps on 28th September, taking over the 3rd and 59th Divisions in line. After relief this corps sector passed to Second Army from Fifth Army.

(viii)[1] SECOND BATTLE OF PASSCHENDAELE, 26TH OCTOBER—10TH NOVEMBER.

Second Army.

II Corps[2] : 1st, 58th and 63rd Divisions.
IX Corps : 19th and 37th Divisions.
X Corps : 5th, 7th, 14th, 21st, 23rd and 39th Divisions.
Canadian Corps : 1st Canadian, 2nd Canadian, 3rd Canadian, and 4th Canadian Divisions.
I Anzac Corps : 1st Australian, 2nd Australian and 5th Australian Divisions.

Fifth Army.

XIV Corps[3] : 35th, 50th and 57th Divisions.
XVIII Corps[2] : 58th and 63rd Divisions.
XIX Corps[3] : 17th, 18th, 35th, 50th and 57th Divisions.

Operations. The Cambrai Operations (20th November—7th December, 1917).

In this battle, as the composition of the corps was continually changing, the system of allotting divisions to corps, as has been done in previous battles, has not been used and the various formations engaged have been grouped together according to type. On the other hand, corps have been shown with their divisions under the heading "Tactical Incidents."

BATTLE OF CAMBRAI, 1917, 20th November—3rd December.

Third Army.[4]

Corps : Cavalry, III, IV, V and VII.
Divisions : 1st Cavalry, 2nd Cavalry, 4th Cavalry, 5th Cavalry, Guards, 2nd, 3rd, 6th, 12th, 20th, 21st, 29th, 36th, 40th, 47th, 51st, 55th, 56th, 59th, 61st and 62nd.
Total number of divisions engaged : 17 and 4 cavalry.

---

[1] The Fifth Army carried out a minor operation on the 22nd October which is not mentioned in the Official Battle List. The following extract from paragraph 59 of Lord Haig's Despatch dated 25th December, 1917, deals with this operation :—

" . . . on 22nd October two successful operations in which we captured over 200 prisoners and gained positions of considerable local importance east of Poelcappelle and within the southern edge of the Houthulst Forest, were undertaken by us . . . ."

The Fifth Army troops engaged were :—
XIV Corps : 34th and 35th Divisions.
XVIII Corps : 18th Division.

[2] II Corps, Second Army relieved XVIII Corps, Fifth Army, on 2nd November, 1917.

[3] XIX Corps relieved the XIV Corps on 29th October, 1917.

[4] The 3rd and 16th Divisions of the VI Corps carried out an important subsidiary attack at Bullecourt on the 20th November, but this action was not within the boundaries of the battle.

Tactical Incidents :

The Tank Attack, 20th—21st November.

Cavalry Corps : 1st Cavalry, 2nd Cavalry and 5th Cavalry Divisions.
III Corps : 6th, 12th, 20th and 29th Divisions.
IV Corps : 36th, 51st, 56th and 62nd Divisions.
VII Corps : 55th Division.

Capture of Bourlon Wood,[1] *23rd—28th November.*

III Corps : 6th, 12th, 20th and 29th Divisions.
IV Corps : 1st Cavalry, 2nd Cavalry, Guards, 2nd, 36th, 40th, 51st, 56th[2] and 62nd Divisions.
VI Corps : 56th[2] Division.
VII Corps : 55th Division.

The German Counter-Attacks, 30th November—3rd *December.*

III Corps : 1st Cavalry, 2nd Cavalry, 4th Cavalry, 5th Cavalry, Guards, 6th, 12th, 20th, 29th, 36th, and 61st Divisions.
IV Corps[3] : 2nd, 47th and 59th Divisions.
V Corps[3] : 2nd, 47th, 51st[4] and 59th Divisions.
VI Corps : 3rd, 51st[4] and 56th Divisions.
VII Corps : 21st and 55th Divisions.

With subsequent—

Action of Welch Ridge, 30th December.

Third Army.

V Corps : 63rd Division.
VII Corps : 9th Division.

---

[1] The boundaries for the Capture of the Bourlon Wood are the same as those for the Tank Attack, so all formations on the battle front qualify for this incident. The fighting that took place actually within Bourlon Wood was carried out by troops of IV Corps.

[2] The 56th Division was transferred from IV Corps to VI Corps on 24th November.

[3] The V Corps relieved the IV Corps on 1st December, 1917, taking over the 2nd, 47th and 59th Divisions in line.

[4] The 51st Division relieved the 56th Division, VI Corps, during night 2/3rd December, and on completion of relief on 3rd December the 51st came under V Corps.

PHASE VI.—THE GERMAN OFFENSIVES, 1918.

Operations. The Offensive in Picardy (21st March—5th April, 1918).

THE FIRST BATTLES OF THE SOMME, 1918, 21ST MARCH—5TH APRIL.

Armies : First, Third, Fourth and Fifth.
Corps : III, IV, V, VI, VII, XIII, XVII, XVIII and XIX.
Divisions : 1st Cavalry (2), 2nd Cavalry (1), 3rd Cavalry (3), Guards (3), 2nd (3), 3rd (3), 4th (1), 6th (1), 8th (3), 9th (2), 12th (3), 14th (2), 15th (2), 16th (2), 17th (2), 18th (2), 19th (2), 20th (3), 21st (2), 24th (4), 25th (2), 30th (3), 31st (3), 32nd (2), 34th (1), 35th (1), 36th (3), 37th (1), 39th (3), 40th (2), 41st (3), 42nd (3), 47th (3), 50th (3), 51st (2), 56th (1), 58th (2), 59th (2), 61st (3), 62nd (2), 63rd (3), 66th (3), 2nd Canadian (1), 2nd Australian (1), 3rd Australian (1), 4th Australian (2), 5th Australian (1), and New Zealand (2).
The 1st Canadian Division came into line on the battle front but did not take part in any specified battle.
Total number of divisions engaged : 46, and 3 cavalry.

(i) BATTLE OF ST. QUENTIN, 21ST—23RD MARCH.

Third Army.

IV Corps : 6th, 19th, 25th, 41st and 51st Divisions.
V Corps : 2nd, 17th, 47th and 63rd Divisions.
VI Corps : Guards, 3rd, 31st, 34th, 40th and 59th Divisions.

Fifth Army.

III Corps : 2nd Cavalry, 3rd Cavalry, 14th, 18th and 58th Divisions.
VII Corps : 9th, 16th, 21st and 39th Divisions.
XVIII Corps : 20th, 30th, 36th and 61st Divisions.
XIX Corps : 1st Cavalry, 8th, 24th, 50th and 66th Divisions.

Actions at the Somme Crossings, 24th—25th March.

Fifth Army.

VII Corps[1] : 39th Division.
XVIII Corps : 3rd Cavalry, 20th, 30th, 36th and 61st Divisions.
XIX Corps : 8th, 24th, 50th and 66th Divisions.

---

[1] The 16th and 39th Divisions of the VII Corps were transferred to XIX Corps on 25th March and the VII Corps came under Third Army.

(ii) First Battle of Bapaume, 1918, 24th—25th March.

Third Army.

IV Corps: 19th, 25th, 41st, 51st and 62nd Divisions.
V Corps: 2nd, 12th (less 37th Infantry Brigade), 17th, 47th and 63rd Divisions.
VI Corps: Guards, 3rd, 31st, 40th, 42nd and 59th Divisions.
XVII Corps: 15th Division.

Fifth Army.

VII Corps: 1st Cavalry, 9th, 21st and 35th Divisions and 37th Infantry Brigade, 12th Division.

(iii) Battle of Rosières, 26th—27th March.

Fifth Army.

XVIII Corps: 20th, 30th, 36th and 61st Divisions.
XIX Corps: 8th, 16th, 24th, 39th, 50th and 66th Divisions and Carey's Force.[1]

(iv) First Battle of Arras, 1918, 28th March.

First Army.

XIII Corps: 56th Division.

Third Army.

IV Corps: 41st, 42nd, 62nd and New Zealand Divisions and 4th Australian Infantry Brigade, 4th Australian Division.
V Corps: 2nd and 12th Divisions.
VI Corps: Guards, 3rd, 31st and 2nd Canadian (2 brigades) Divisions and 97th Infantry Brigade, 32nd Division.
XVII Corps: 4th and 15th Divisions.

(v) Battle of the Avre, 4th April.

Fourth Army.[2]

XIX Corps: 3rd Cavalry, 14th, 18th, 24th, and 58th Divisions, 5th Australian Infantry Brigade, 2nd Australian Division; 9th Australian Infantry Brigade, 3rd Australian Division; 8th and 15th Australian Infantry Brigades, 5th Australian Division.

---

[1] A composite force, formed from various details, schools, R.E. units and some American Engineers, was collected by Fifth Army Staff on 25th March, placed in position by Major-General P. G. Grant, C.E., Fifth Army, and taken over by Major-General G. G. S. Carey, who was on his way to take over the command of the 20th Division, on the afternoon of 26th March. This force, now known as Carey's Force, was relieved during the night 2/3 April.

[2] The reconstituted Fourth Army H.Q. took over from Fifth Army H.Q. on 2nd April and the Fifth Army became the Reserve Army.

(vi) BATTLE OF THE ANCRE, 1918, 5TH APRIL.

Third Army.

IV Corps: 37th, 42nd and New Zealand Divisions and 4th Australian Infantry Brigade, 4th Australian Division.
V Corps: 12th, 47th and 63rd Divisions.
VI Corps: 32nd Division.
VII Corps: 4th Australian Division (12th and 13th Australian Infantry Brigades).

With subsequent—

(i) *Actions of Villers Bretonneux, 24th—25th April.*

Fourth Army.

III Corps: 8th, 18th and 58th Divisions.
Australian Corps[1]: 4th Australian and 5th Australian Divisions.

(ii) *Capture of Hamel, 4th July.*

Fourth Army.

Australian Corps: 4th Australian Division (4th Australian Infantry Brigade); 6th Australian Infantry Brigade, 2nd Australian Division; 11th Australian Infantry Brigade, 3rd Australian Division.

Two companies each from the 131st and 132nd Infantry Regiments, 33rd American Division.

All the above troops were under the orders of the 4th Australian Division for the operation.

Operations. The Offensive in Flanders (9th—29th April, 1918).

THE BATTLES OF THE LYS, 9TH—29TH APRIL.

Armies: First and Second.
Corps: I, IX, XI, XV and XXII.
Divisions: 1st (3), 3rd (3), 4th (2), 5th (1), 6th (4), 9th (5), 19th (3), 21st (4), 25th (6), 29th (5), 30th (3), 31st (2), 33rd (4), 34th (5), 36th (3), 39th (3), 40th (2), 49th (5), 50th (2), 51st (1), 55th (2), 59th (2), 61st (3) and 1st Australian (1).

2nd Portuguese (1) *and 3rd Infantry Brigade, 1st Portuguese* (1).

The XIII Corps and the 46th Division came into line on the battle front but did not take part in any specified battle.
Total number of divisions engaged: 25 and 1 *Portuguese.*

---

[1] On 31st December, 1917, the I Anzac Corps became the Australian Corps, and the II Anzac Corps became the XXII Corps.

(i) Battle of Estaires, 9th—11th April.

First Army.

XI Corps: 3rd, 51st, 55th, and 61st Divisions and 2nd Infantry Brigade, 1st Division, *2nd Portuguese Division and 3rd Infantry Brigade, 1st Portuguese Division.*

XV Corps: 29th (86th and 87th Infantry Brigades), 31st, 34th,[1] 40th and 50th Divisions and 74th Infantry Brigade, 25th Division.

Tactical Incidents:

First Defence of Givenchy, 1918: 55th Division.

(ii) Battle of Messines, 1918, 10th—11th April.

Second Army.

IX Corps: 9th, 19th and 25th (less 74th Infantry Brigade) Divisions; 62nd Infantry Brigade, 21st Division; 88th Infantry Brigade, 29th Division; 100th Infantry Brigade, 33rd Division; 102nd Infantry Brigade, 34th Division; 108th Infantry Brigade, 36th Division; 147th and 148th Infantry Brigades, 49th Division.

(iii) Battle of Hazebrouck, 12th—15th April.

First Army.

I Corps[2]: 3rd, 4th and 55th Divisions and 3rd Infantry Brigade, 1st Division.

XI Corps: 5th, 50th and 61st Division.

XV Corps[3]: 29th (86th and 87th Infantry Brigades), 31st, 33rd, 40th and 1st Australian Divisions and Composite Force.[4]

Tactical Incidents:

Defence of Hinges Ridge: 3rd, 4th, 51st and 61st Divisions.

Defence of Nieppe Forest: 5th, 29th, 31st and 1st Australian Divisions.

---

[1] A portion of the 34th Division, 102nd Infantry Brigade, was fighting in the Second Army area from 10th April (see IX Corps, Battle of Messines, 1918).

[2] It appears that the 1st and 55th Divisions do not officially qualify for this battle as they were east of the River Lawe, the right battle boundary; but as their fighting on these days was clearly part of this battle they have been added.

[3] The XV Corps was transferred to Second Army at noon, 12th April.

[4] This force was apparently composed as follows:—
Personnel from II and XXII Corps School.
2/New Zealand Entrenching Bn.
2 coys. 18/Middlesex R. (Pioneers).
XXII Corps Reinforcement Bn.

(iv) BATTLE OF BAILLEUL, 13TH—15TH APRIL.

Second Army.

IX Corps: 19th, 25th, 34th, 49th and 59th Divisions; 71st Infantry Brigade, 6th Division; South African Infantry Brigade, 9th Division; 88th Infantry Brigade, 29th Division; 100th Infantry Brigade, 33rd Division; 108th Infantry Brigade, 36th Division.

XXII Corps: 9th Division.

Tactical Incidents:

Defence of Neuve Eglise: 33rd and 49th Divisions.

(v) FIRST BATTLE OF KEMMEL, 17TH—19TH APRIL.

Second Army.[1]

IX Corps: 19th, 25th, 33rd, 34th, 49th and 59th Divisions; 71st Infantry Brigade, 6th Division; 88th Infantry Brigade, 29th Division; 89th Brigade, 30th Division; 108th Infantry Brigade, 36th Division; Wyatt's Force.[2]

XXII Corps: 9th and 39th[3] Divisions and 62nd and 64th Infantry Brigades, 21st Division.

(vi) BATTLE OF BÉTHUNE, 18TH APRIL.

First Army.

I Corps: 1st, 3rd and 4th Divisions.

XI Corps: 61st Division.

Tactical Incidents:

Second Defence of Givenchy, 1918: 1st Division.

(vii) SECOND BATTLE OF KEMMEL, 25TH—26TH APRIL.

Second Army.

XXII Corps: 9th, 21st, 25th,[4] 39th and 49th Divisions and 71st Infantry Brigade, 6th Division and 89th Infantry Brigade, 30th Division.

---

[1] The *II (French) Cavalry Corps* and the *XXXVI (French) Corps* were arriving in the battle area of the IX Corps throughout this battle.

[2] Wyatt's Force, some 1,500 strong, was formed from various details and miscellaneous units in the IX Corps and was commanded by Brigadier-General L. J. Wyatt of the 116th Infantry Brigade, 39th Division.

[3] The 39th Division was organised as a composite brigade for these battles.

[4] On 25th April the *XXXVI (French) Corps* and the *II (French) Cavalry Corps* were holding the southern part of the battle front from north-west of Bailleul to 2,000 yards west-south-west of Wytschaete. The *II (French) Cavalry Corps*, to which were attached the 456th Field Coy., R.E., the 19/Lancashire Fusiliers and part of the 49th Bn. M.G.C., all of 49th Division, held that part of the line in front of Mont Kemmel. The Germans, after a heavy gas shell bombardment, drove the *28th (French) Division* off Mont Kemmel about 9 a.m. The 25th Division, then resting in the Poperinghe-Proven area, was ordered to proceed to the help of the French, and the three infantry brigades were in the Reninghelst area by 5 p.m. The 25th Division carried out a counter-attack at 3 a.m. on the next day, 26th April, and was later transferred to XXII Corps.

Détachment d'armée du Nord.

II (French) Cavalry Corps: 28th, 39th and 154th (French) Divisions and 3rd (French) Cavalry Division.

XXXVI (French) Corps: 34th and 133rd (French) Divisions and 2nd (French) Cavalry Division.

(viii) BATTLE OF THE SCHERPENBERG, 29TH APRIL.

Second Army.

XXII Corps: 6th, 21st, 25th, 39th and 49th Divisions and South African Infantry Brigade, 9th Division and 89th Infantry Brigade, 30th Division.

Détachment d'armée du Nord.

II (French) Cavalry Corps: 39th and 154th (French) Divisions and 2nd and 3rd (French) Cavalry Divisions.

XXXVI (French) Corps: 34th Division.

With subsequent—

(i) *Action of La Becque, 28th June.*

First Army.

XI Corps: 5th Division.

Second Army.

XV Corps[1]: 31st Division.

(ii) *Capture of Meteren, 19th July.*

Second Army.

XV Corps: 9th Division.

Operations. The Offensive in Champagne (27th May—6th June 1918).

BATTLE OF THE AISNE, 1918, 27th May—6th June.

IX Corps: 8th, 19th,[2] 21st, 25th and 50th Divisions.

The IX Corps was under the *Sixth (French) Army* until 28th June, when it was transferred to the *Fifth (French) Army*. On 30th June the IX Corps was withdrawn from the battle and the British troops remaining in line, 19th Division, with elements of the other four divisions, came under the *V (French) Corps*.

---

[1] The 31st Division was lent to XI Corps for this Action in order that the operation might be under one Commander.

[2] On 27th May, 1918, the 19th Division was in reserve in the area Châlons-Vitry le François and under the command of the VIII Corps, which was in reserve to the *Fourth (French) Army*. The division moved up to the line during night 28/29 May in buses and came under IX Corps.

PHASE VII.—THE ADVANCE TO VICTORY, 1918.

Operations. The Counter-Attack in Champagne (20th July—2nd August, 1918).

THE BATTLES OF THE MARNE, 1918, 20TH JULY—2ND AUGUST.

Corps : XXII.
Divisions : 15th (1), 34th (1), 51st (1), and 62nd (1).

(i) BATTLE OF THE SOISSONAIS AND OF THE OURCQ, 23RD JULY—2ND AUGUST.

15th Division under *XX (French) Corps.*
34th Division under *XXX (French) Corps.*

Tactical Incidents :

Attack on Buzancy (28th July) : 15th Division.
Capture of the Beugneux Ridge : 34th Division.

(ii) BATTLE OF TARDENOIS, 20TH—31ST JULY.

XXII Corps : 51st and 62nd Divisions.

Tactical Incidents :

The fighting for the Ardre Valley : 51st and 62nd Divisions.

The XXII Corps was under the *Fifth (French) Army.*

Operations. The Advance in Picardy (8th August—3rd September, 1918).

THE BATTLE OF AMIENS, 8TH—11TH AUGUST.

Fourth Army.

Cavalry Corps : 1st Cavalry, 2nd Cavalry and 3rd Cavalry Divisions.

III Corps : 12th, 18th, 47th[1] and 58th Divisions *and 130th and 131st*[2] *Infantry Regiments of 33rd American Division.*

Canadian Corps : 32nd, 1st Canadian, 2nd Canadian, 3rd Canadian and 4th Canadian Divisions.

---

[1] The 47th Division, with 130*th American Infantry Regiment* attached, did not actually attack in this battle but technically qualifies as the right of the division was within the geographical limits of the battle.

[2] The 131*st American Infantry Regiment* was transferred from III Corps to Australian Corps on 9th August.

Australian Corps: 17th, 1st Australian, 2nd Australian, 3rd Australian, 4th Australian and 5th Australian Divisions.

131st[1] Infantry Regiment, 33rd American Division.

With subsequent—

Actions round Damery, 15th—17th August.

Fourth Army.

Canadian Corps: 1st Canadian, 2nd Canadian, 3rd Canadian and 4th Canadian Divisions.

THE SECOND BATTLES OF THE SOMME, 1918, 21ST AUGUST—3RD SEPTEMBER.

Armies: Third and Fourth.
Corps: III, IV, V, VI and Australian.
Divisions: Guards (2), 2nd (2), 3rd (2), 5th (2), 12th (1), 17th (2), 18th (2), 21st (2), 32nd (2), 37th (1), 38th (2), 42nd (2), 47th (2), 52nd (1), 56th (1), 58th (2), 59th (1) 62nd (1), 63rd (1), 74th (1), 1st Australian (1), 2nd Australian (1), 3rd Australian (2), 4th Australian (1), 5th Australian (2), and New Zealand (2).
Total number of divisions engaged: 26.

(i) BATTLE OF ALBERT, 1918, 21ST—23RD AUGUST.

Third Army.

IV Corps: 5th, 37th, 42nd, 63rd and New Zealand Divisions.
V Corps: 17th, 21st and 38th Divisions.
VI Corps: Guards, 2nd, 3rd, 52nd, 56th and 59th Divisions.

Fourth Army.

III Corps: 12th, 18th, 47th and 58th Divisions.
Australian Corps: 32nd, 1st Australian, 3rd Australian, 4th Australian and 5th Australian Divisions.

Tactical Incidents:

Capture of Chuignes: 1st Australian Division.

(ii) SECOND BATTLE OF BAPAUME, 1918, 31ST AUGUST—3RD SEPTEMBER.

Third Army.

IV Corps: 5th, 42nd and New Zealand Divisions.
V Corps: 17th, 21st and 38th Divisions.
VI Corps: Guards, 2nd, 3rd and 62nd Divisions.

Fourth Army.

III Corps: 18th, 47th, 58th and 74th Divisions.
Australian Corps: 32nd, 2nd Australian, 3rd Australian and 5th Australian Divisions.

Tactical Incidents:

Capture of Mont St. Quentin: 2nd Australian Division.

Miscellaneous Incidents:

Occupation of Péronne: 5th Australian Division.

---

[1] *See* footnote 2, page 32.

Operations. The Advance in Flanders (18th August—6th September, 1918).[1]

Second Army.

X Corps: 30th and 36th Divisions.
XV Corps: 9th, 29th, 31st and 40th Divisions.
XIX Corps: 6th, 34th and 41st Divisions, *and 27th American Division.*

Fifth Army.

XI Corps: 59th, 61st and 74th Divisions.
XIII Corps: 4th, 19th and 46th Divisions.

Action of Outtersteene Ridge, 18th August.

Second Army.

XV Corps: 9th and 29th Divisions.

Operations. The Breaking of the Hindenburg Line (26th August—12th October, 1918).

THE SECOND BATTLES OF ARRAS, 1918, 26TH AUGUST—3RD SEPTEMBER.

Armies: First and Third.
Corps: VIII, XVII, XXII and Canadian.
Divisions: 1st (1), 4th (2), 8th (1), 11th (2), 51st (1), 52nd (2), 56th (1), 57th (2), 63rd (1), 1st Canadian (2), 2nd Canadian (1), 3rd Canadian (1), and 4th Canadian (1).
Also Brutinel's Brigade (2).
Total number of divisions engaged: 13.

(i) BATTLE OF THE SCARPE, 1918, 26TH—30TH AUGUST.

First Army

VIII Corps[2]: 8th Division (25th Infantry Brigade).
XXII Corps[3]: 11th and 51st Divisions.
Canadian Corps: 4th, 51st, 1st Canadian, 2nd Canadian and 3rd Canadian Divisions and Brutinel's Brigade.[4]

---

[1] The 55th Division, I Corps, First Army, commenced to join in this advance at the end of August.

[2] The VIII Corps came within the geographical limits of the battle on 28th August when the 8th Division relieved part of 51st Division, Canadian Corps.

[3] The XXII Corps came in on 29th August, taking over 51st Division from Canadian Corps.

[4] Brutinel's Brigade was a force formed in the Canadian Corps under the orders of Brig.-Gen. R. Brutinel and was composed as follows:—

1st and 2nd Canadian Motor Machine Gun Brigades.
Canadian Corps Cyclist Battalion.
One section of six-inch Newton Trench Mortars mounted on lorries.

It fought in the Battle of Amiens in the Canadian Corps under the name of the Canadian Independent Force.

Third Army.

XVII Corps: 52nd, 56th and 57th Divisions.

Tactical Incidents:

Capture of Monchy le Preux: 3rd Canadian Division.

(ii) BATTLE OF DROCOURT-QUÉANT, 2ND—3RD SEPTEMBER.

First Army.

XXII Corps: 11th Division (less 34th Infantry Brigade).
Canadian Corps: 1st, 4th, 1st Canadian and 4th Canadian Divisions and Brutinel's Brigade.[1]

Third Army.

XVII Corps: 52nd, 57th and 63rd Divisions.

THE BATTLES OF THE HINDENBURG LINE, 12TH SEPTEMBER—9TH OCTOBER.

Armies: First, Third and Fourth.
Corps: Cavalry, III, IV, V, VI, VIII, IX, XIII, XVII, XXII, Canadian, Australian and *II American*.
Divisions: 1st Cavalry (1), 2nd Cavalry (1), 3rd Cavalry (1), Guards (3), 1st (3), 2nd (3), 3rd (2), 4th (1), 5th (2), 6th (4), 11th (2), 12th (2), 17th (3), 18th (2), 21st (3), 24th (1), 25th (2), 32nd (2), 33rd (2), 37th (3), 38th (4), 42nd (1), 46th (3), 50th (3), 52nd (1), 56th (2), 57th (2), 58th (1), 62nd (2), 63rd (2), 66th (1), 74th (1), 1st Canadian (2), 2nd Canadian (1), 3rd Canadian (2), 4th Canadian (1), 1st Australian (1), 2nd Australian (2), 3rd Australian (1), 4th Australian (1), 5th Australian (1) and New Zealand (3), *27th American* (1) *and 30th American* (2).
Also Brutinel's Brigade (2).
Total number of divisions engaged: 39, 3 cavalry and 2 *American*.

(i) BATTLE OF HAVRINCOURT, 12TH SEPTEMBER.

Third Army.

IV Corps: 37th and New Zealand Divisions.
V Corps: 17th and 38th Divisions.
VI Corps: Guards, 2nd and 62nd Divisions.

(ii) BATTLE OF EPÉHY, 18TH SEPTEMBER.

Third Army.

IV Corps: 5th Division.
V Corps: 17th, 21st and 38th Divisions.

---

[1] The 10th Hussars (3rd Cavalry Division) were attached to Brutinel's Brigade for this battle.

Fourth Army.

III Corps: 12th, 18th, 58th and 74th Divisions.
IX Corps: 1st and 6th Divisions.
Australian Corps: 1st Australian and 4th Australian Divisions.

(iii) Battle of the Canal du Nord, 27th September—1st October.

First Army.

XXII Corps: 4th[1] and 56th Divisions.
Canadian Corps: 11th, 1st Canadian, 3rd Canadian and 4th Canadian Divisions and Brutinel's Brigade.

Third Army.

IV Corps: 5th, 37th, 42nd and New Zealand Divisions.
VI Corps: Guards, 2nd, 3rd and 62nd Divisions.
XVII Corps: 52nd, 57th and 63rd Divisions.

Tactical Incidents:

Capture of Bourlon Wood: 3rd Canadian Division with 57th and 4th Canadian on the flanks.

(iv) Battle of the St. Quentin Canal, 29th September—2nd October.

Third Army.

V Corps: 21st and 33rd Divisions.

Fourth Army.

III Corps: 12th and 18th Divisions.
IX Corps: 1st, 6th, 32nd and 46th Divisions.
XIII Corps[2]: 18th and 50th Divisions.
Australian Corps[3]: 2nd Australian, 3rd Australian and 5th Australian Divisions and *27th American and 30th American Divisions.*

Tactical Incidents:

Passage at Bellenglise: 46th Division.
Capture of Bellicourt Tunnel Defences: 5th Australian Division and 30*th American Division.*

(v) Battle of Beaurevoir, 3rd—5th October.

Third Army.

V Corps: 38th Division.

---

[1] 4th Division came within the geographical limits of the battle on 1st October.

[2] The XIII Corps relieved the III Corps on 1st October, taking over the 18th Division in line.

[3] The Headquarters of the Australian and *II American Corps* were amalgamated for the first part of this battle, the Australian Corps being in command. The *II American Corps* was withdrawn on 30th September.

Fourth Army.

IX Corps: 6th, 32nd and 46th Divisions and 3rd Infantry Brigade, 1st Division.
XIII Corps: 25th and 50th Divisions.
Australian Corps: 2nd Australian Division.

(vi) BATTLE OF CAMBRAI, 1918, 8TH—9TH OCTOBER.

First Army.

XXII Corps: 56th and 1st Canadian Divisions.
Canadian Corps: 11th, 2nd Canadian and 3rd Canadian Divisions and Brutinel's Brigade.

Third Army.

2nd Cavalry Division (less 5th Cavalry Brigade).
IV Corps: 37th and New Zealand Divisions.
V Corps: 17th, 21st, 33rd and 38th Divisions.
VI Corps: Guards, 2nd and 3rd Divisions.
XVII Corps: 24th, 57th and 63rd Divisions.

Fourth Army.

Cavalry Corps: 1st Cavalry and 3rd Cavalry Divisions.
IX Corps: 6th and 46th Divisions and 5th Cavalry Brigade, 2nd Cavalry Division.
XIII Corps: 25th, 50th and 66th Divisions.
II American Corps: *30th American Division.*

Tactical Incidents:

Capture of Villers Outréaux: 38th Division.
Capture of Cambrai: 57th and 3rd Canadian Divisions.

Operations. The Pursuit to the Selle[1] (9th—12th October).

First Army.

XXII Corps[2]: 49th, 51st, 56th and 2nd Canadian Divisions.
Canadian Corps[2]: 11th, 49th, 56th and 2nd Canadian Divisions.

---

[1] As no boundaries have been assigned to these Operations all formations in line between the *First French Army* and the Sensée River have been shown in the general list.

[2] The XXII and Canadian Corps exchanged fronts on 11th October, 1918, when the 56th Division was transferred from XXII Corps to Canadian and the 49th and 2nd Canadian Divisions from the Canadian Corps to the XXII.

Diagrammatically the change was as follows:—

Before: 1st Can. Div. 56th Div. 11th Div. 2nd Can. Div. 49th Div.
XXII Corps. Canadian Corps.
After: 1st Can. Div. 56th Div. 11th Div. 2nd Can. Div. 49th Div.
Canadian Corps. XXII Corps.

The 1st Canadian Division was outside the limits of the operations.

Third Army.

2nd Cavalry Division (less 5th Cavalry Brigade).
IV Corps : 5th, 37th, 42nd and New Zealand Divisions.
V Corps : 17th and 33rd Divisions.
VI Corps : Guards Division.
XVII Corps : 24th Division.

Fourth Army.

Cavalry Corps : 1st Cavalry and 3rd Cavalry Divisions.
IX Corps : 6th and 46th Divisions and 5th Cavalry Brigade, 2nd Cavalry Division.
XIII Corps : 25th, 50th and 66th Divisions.
II American Corps : 27th American and 30th American Divisions.

Operations. The Final Advance—Flanders (28th September—11th November).

BATTLE OF YPRES, 1918, 28th September—2nd October.

Second Army.

II Corps : 9th, 29th and 36th Divisions.
X Corps : 30th and 34th Divisions.
XV Corps : 31st and 40th Divisions.
XIX Corps : 14th, 35th and 41st Divisions.

BATTLE OF COURTRAI, 14th—19th October.

Second Army.

II Corps : 9th, 29th and 36th Divisions.
X Corps : 30th and 34th Divisions.
XV Corps : 14th Division.
XIX Corps : 35th and 41st Divisions.

With subsequent—

(i) *Action of Ooteghem, 25th October.*

Second Army.

II Corps : 9th and 36th Divisions.
X Corps : 34th Divisions.
XIX Corps : 41st Division.

(ii) *Action of Tieghem, 31st October.*

Second Army.

II Corps : 31st and 34th Divisions.
XIX Corps : 35th Division.

Operations. The Final Advance—Artois[1] (2nd October—11th November).

First Army.

VIII Corps: 8th, 12th, 52nd, and 58th[2] Divisions.

Fifth Army.

I Corps: 15th, 16th, 55th and 58th[2] Divisions.
III Corps[3]: 55th and 74th Divisions.
XI Corps: 47th, 57th, 61st and 74th Divisions.

Capture of Douai, 17th October.

First Army.

VIII Corps: 8th Division.

Operations. The Final Advance—Picardy (17th October—11th November).

BATTLE OF THE SELLE, 17th—25th October.

First Army.

XXII Corps: 4th, 49th, and 51st Divisions.

Third Army.

IV Corps: 5th, 37th, 42nd and New Zealand Divisions.
V Corps: 17th, 21st, 33rd and 38th Divisions.
VI Corps: Guards, 2nd, 3rd and 62nd Divisions.
XVII Corps: 19th and 61st Divisions.

Fourth Army.

IX Corps: 1st, 6th and 46th Divisions.
XIII Corps: 18th, 25th, 50th and 66th Divisions.
II American Corps: 27th American and 30th American Divisions

BATTLE OF VALENCIENNES, 1st—2nd November.

First Army.

XXII Corps: 4th and 49th Divisions.
Canadian Corps: 3rd Canadian and 4th Canadian Divisions.

---

[1] Here again no boundaries have been fixed. The compiler has treated these Operations as the connecting link between the southern and northern wings of the British offensive and all formations in line between the left corps (XXII till 11th October, then Canadian) of the southern attacks and the right corps (XV) of the northern attacks have been given.

[2] 58th Division was transferred from VIII Corps, First Army, to I Corps, Fifth Army, on 14th October, 1918.

[3] The III Corps came into line on the 8th October, 1918, between the I and XI Corps, taking over the 55th Division from the former and the 74th Division from the latter.

Third Army.

XVII Corps: 19th, 24th and 61st Divisions.

Tactical Incidents:

Capture of Mont Houy: 4th Canadian Division.

BATTLE OF THE SAMBRE, 4th November.

First Army.

XXII Corps: 11th and 56th Divisions.
Canadian Corps: 4th Canadian Division.

Third Army.

2nd Cavalry Division (less 5th Cavalry Brigade).
IV Corps: 37th and New Zealand Divisions.
V Corps: 17th and 38th Divisions.
VI Corps: Guards and 62nd Divisions.
XVII Corps: 19th and 24th Divisions.

Fourth Army.

IX Corps: 1st and 32nd Divisions and 5th Cavalry Brigade, 2nd Cavalry Division.
XIII Corps: 18th, 25th and 50th Divisions.

Tactical Incidents:

Passage of the Sambre-Oise Canal: 1st, 25th and 32nd Divisions.
Capture of Le Quesnoy: New Zealand Division.

And subsequent—

(i) *Passage of the Grande Honelle, 5th—7th November.*

First Army.

XXII Corps: 11th, 56th and 63rd Divisions.
Canadian Corps: 2nd Canadian and 4th Canadian Divisions.

Third Army.

XVII Corps: 19th and 24th Divisions.

(ii) *Capture of Mons, 11th November.*

First Army.

Canadian Corps: 3rd Canadian Division.

APPENDIX

TABLE SHOWING EACH DIVISION'S SERVICE IN FRANCE AND FLANDERS

Division.	Served in France and Flanders		Remarks.
	From	To	
1st Cavalry (Regular) ...	Aug., 1914	Armistice	
2nd Cavalry (Regular) ...	Sept., 1914	Armistice	Formed in France.
3rd Cavalry (Regular) ...	Oct., 1914	Armistice	
4th Cavalry (Indian) ...	Oct., 1914	Feb., 1918	See Note 1.
5th Cavalry (Indian) ...	Dec., 1914	Feb., 1918	See Note 1.
Guards (Regular)	Aug., 1915	Armistice	Formed in France.
1st (Regular)	Aug., 1914	Armistice	
2nd (Regular)	Aug., 1914	Armistice	
3rd (Regular)	Aug., 1914	Armistice	
4th (Regular)	Aug., 1914	Armistice	
5th (Regular) ...	Aug., 1914	Nov., 1917	
	April, 1918	Armistice	
6th (Regular)	Sept., 1914	Armistice	
7th (Regular)	Oct., 1914	Armistice	
8th (Regular)	Nov., 1914	Armistice	
9th (Scottish) (New Army)	May, 1915	Armistice	
11th (Northern) (New Army)	July, 1916	Armistice	
12th (Eastern) (New Army)	May, 1915	Armistice	
14th (Light) (New Army) ...	May, 1915	Armistice	See Note 2.
15th (Scottish) (New Army)	July, 1915	Armistice	
16th (Irish) (New Army) ...	Dec., 1915	Armistice	See Note 3.
17th (Northern) (New Army)	July, 1915	Armistice	
18th (Eastern) (New Army)	July, 1915	Armistice	
19th (Western) (New Army)	July, 1915	Armistice	
20th (Light) (New Army) ...	July, 1915	Armistice	
21st (New Army)	Sept., 1915	Armistice	
22nd (New Army)	Sept., 1915	Nov., 1915	
23rd (New Army)	Aug., 1915	Nov., 1917	
24th (New Army)	Aug., 1915	Armistice	
25th (New Army)	Sept., 1915	Armistice	See Note 4.
27th (Regular)	Dec., 1914	Nov., 1915	
28th (Regular)	Jan., 1915	Nov., 1915	
29th (Regular)	Mar., 1916	Armistice	
30th (New Army)	Nov., 1915	Armistice	See Note 5.
31st (New Army)	Mar., 1916	Armistice	
32nd (New Army)	Nov., 1915	Armistice	
33rd (New Army)	Nov., 1915	Armistice	
34th (New Army)	Jan., 1916	Armistice	See Note 6.
35th (New Army)	Jan., 1916	Armistice	
36th (Ulster) (New Army) ...	Oct., 1915	Armistice	
37th (New Army)	July, 1915	Armistice	
38th (Welsh) (New Army) ...	Dec., 1915	Armistice	
39th (New Army)	Mar., 1916	Armistice	See Note 7.
40th (New Army)	June, 1916	Armistice	See Note 8.
41st (New Army) ...	May, 1916	Nov., 1917	
	Mar., 1918	Armistice	
42nd (East Lancashire) T.F.	Mar., 1917	Armistice	
46th (North Midland) T.F.	Feb., 1915	Armistice	See Note 9.

Division.	Served in France and Flanders		Remarks.
	From	To	
47th (2nd London) T.F. ...	Mar., 1915	Armistice	
48th (South Midland) T.F.	Mar., 1915	Nov., 1917	
49th (West Riding) T.F. ...	April, 1915	Armistice	
50th (Northumbrian) T.F. ...	April, 1915	Armistice	See Note 10.
51st (Highland) T.F. ...	April, 1915	Armistice	
52nd (Lowland) T.F. ...	April, 1918	Armistice	
55th (West Lancashire) T.F.	Jan., 1916	Armistice	Assembled in France
56th (1st London) T.F. ...	Jan., 1916	Armistice	Assembled in France
57th (2/West Lancashire) T.F.	Feb., 1917	Armistice	
58th (2/1st London) T.F. ...	Jan., 1917	Armistice	
59th (2/North Midland) T.F.	Feb., 1917	Armistice	See Note 11.
60th (2/2nd London) T.F. ...	June, 1916	Nov., 1916	
61st (2/South Midland) T.F.	May, 1916	Armistice	
62nd (2/West Riding) T.F.	Jan., 1917	Armistice	
63rd (Royal Naval) ...	May, 1916	Armistice	See Note 12.
66th (2/E. Lancashire) T.F.	Mar., 1917	Armistice	See Note 13.
74th (Yeomanry)	May, 1918	Armistice	
3rd Indian (Lahore) ...	Sept., 1914	Dec., 1915	
7th Indian (Meerut) ...	Oct., 1914	Dec., 1915	
1st Canadian	Feb., 1915	Armistice	
2nd Canadian	Sept., 1915	Armistice	
3rd Canadian	Jan., 1916	Armistice	Formed in France.
4th Canadian	Aug., 1916	Armistice	
1st Australian	Mar., 1916	Armistice	
2nd Australian	Mar., 1916	Armistice	
3rd Australian	Nov., 1916	Armistice	
4th Australian	June, 1916	Armistice	
5th Australian	June, 1916	Armistice	
New Zealand	April, 1916	Armistice	

Note 1.—The 4th and 5th Cavalry Divisions were originally the 1st and 2nd Indian Cavalry Divisions. (See footnote, p. 16.)

Note 2.—The 14th Division was reduced to cadre in April, 1918, returned to England in June, and, after being reconstituted with fresh battalions, went back to France in July, 1918.

Note 3.—The 16th Division was reduced to cadre in April, 1918, returned to England in June, and was reconstituted with 5 English, 2 Scottish, 1 Welsh, and 1 Irish battalions, returning to France in July/August, 1918.

Note 4.—The 25th Division was reduced to cadre in June, 1918, and proceeded to England, where, in July, the cadre battalions were made up with drafts. In August the Division made up one full strength brigade for service in North Russia, and the remaining battalions were broken up. The Divisional and Brigade Headquarters returned to France in September, 1918, and the Division was again reconstituted with nine battalions from Italy.

Note 5.—The 30th Division was reduced to cadre in May, 1918, and reconstituted with battalions from other divisions, including five from Palestine, in late June, 1918.

Note 6.—The 34th Division was reduced to cadre in May, 1918, and reconstituted in June with battalions from Palestine.

Note 7.—The 39th Division was reduced to cadre in May, 1918, and was not reconstituted.

Note 8.—The 40th Division was reduced to cadre in May, 1918, and reconstituted with low category battalions in June, 1918.

Note 9.—The 46th Division commenced to move to Egypt in January, 1916, and after Divisional Headquarters and two Infantry Brigades had arrived there the move was cancelled and the whole Division was in France again by the middle of February, 1916.

Note 10.—The 50th Division was reduced to cadre in June, 1918, and was reconstituted in July, 1918, with eight battalions from Salonika and two from another division in France.

Note 11.—The 59th Division was reduced to cadre in May, 1918, and was reconstituted with low category battalions in June.

Note 12.—The 63rd Division served at Antwerp in October, 1914. It was then known as the Royal Naval Division; it received the number 63rd in July, 1916.

Note 13.—The 66th Division was reduced to cadre in May, 1918, and was reconstituted in July/September, 1918, with the South African Brigade, two battalions from the old 66th Division, four from Salonika, and one from the old 30th Division.

N.B.—In the above notes it will be observed that ten divisions were reduced to cadre in 1918; this reduction affected only the infantry battalions. The artillery, engineers, machine-gun battalions, and other divisional troops of these divisions were attached to other formations, until the infantry battalions of their own divisions were reconstituted.

INDEX OF PLACE NAMES

INDEX OF FORMATIONS